Whitby & Pickering Railway

A "Dalesman" Paperback: 8s. 6d.

$(42\frac{1}{2}\text{p.})$

Whitby and Pickering Railway

by
DAVID JOY

**In collaboration with the North Yorkshire Moors Railway
Preservation Society.**

DALESMAN PUBLISHING COMPANY, LTD.
Clapham (via Lancaster)
Yorkshire.
1969

Uniform with this volume:

CUMBRIAN COAST RAILWAYS
MAIN LINE OVER SHAP
SETTLE-CARLISLE RAILWAY (A Revised Edition)
TRANSPORT IN YORKSHIRE

"Dalesman" books on North Yorkshire:

THE CLEVELAND WAY
ESKDALE
LYKE WAKE WALK
RYEDALE AND THE VALE OF PICKERING
YORKSHIRE COAST
YORKSHIRE PORTS AND HARBOURS

Printed and bound in Great Britain by
FRETWELL & BRIAN LTD.
Silsden, Nr. Keighley, Yorkshire.

Contents

Acknowledgements

THE author would especially like to thank G. D. Calvert, Archivist to the North Yorkshire Moors Railway Preservation Society, for help in many ways including reading the manuscript in draft and assisting in the preparation of maps. Other members of the preservation society who have read the book in manuscript form are John Megson, treasurer, and John Tindale, press officer. Invaluable assistance has been given by K. Hoole in locating illustrations.

Much additional help has been given by:- Harold D. Bowtell, John M. Boyes, British Railways Eastern Region, P. Burnett (Librarian, Whitby Literary & Philosophical Society), Mrs. G. E. Deakin, D. Hardy, T. Horn, Dorothy M. Hudson (County Librarian, North Riding County Library), T. E. Rounthwaite, T. Salmon (Secretary, N.Y.M.R.P.S.), W. Eglon Shaw (The Sutcliffe Gallery), W. H. Tate, P. Wilson.

The colour photograph on the front cover of Goathland station was taken in August 1969 by John Tindale (Tindale's of Whitby), and shows left to right: the diesel railbus; No. 3, a Borrows well-tank; *Mirvale*. The illustration on the back cover of a horse-drawn coach crossing one of the original timber bridges over the Esk is from *The Scenery of The Whitby and Pickering Railway* (1836). Other uncredited photographs are:- Title page: Snowy view from cab of diesel unit in Grosmont station (Tindale's of Whitby). Page 3: Bleak prospect near Levisham in February 1964 (D. Hardy). Opposite: Newtondale (collection of H. C. Casserley).

The line and its setting. The Whitby and Pickering Railway writhes like a snake along the green floor of Newtondale, a classic ice-age gorge cutting through the heart of the North York Moors. (Geoffrey N. Wright)

Early Days

WHITBY was worried. The whaling industry which for so long had been the mainstay of the port was in abrupt decline. Alum workings at nearby Saltwick Nab and Sandsend had fallen on hard times, while local shipbuilding was employing only a tenth of its former labour force owing to competition from the more advanced yards of Tees-side and Tyneside. Frustration was increased by the fact that surrounding forests were yielding useful quantities of timber, stone quarrying had begun at Goathland and limestone was being worked in the direction of Pickering, but in all three cases development was being hindered by lack of direct communications.

It was in this era of uncertainty that Whitby, then a railwayless town, saw one of the most significant meetings in railway history. In 1834 George Hudson, who had recently inherited the fortune which was to send him from rags to riches and back to rags in little more than a decade, came to the old seaport to inspect some property which formed part of his legacy. By chance "the railway king" met "the father of railways," George Stephenson, 19 years his senior. Despite the age difference the two men struck up a firm friendship which in the years of railway speculation that lay ahead was to see the younger George promoting vast schemes of expansion while "Old George" took up their execution with equal zeal.

But as yet the "railway mania" belonged firmly to the future. It was a relatively insignificant project—the construction of a horse tramroad from Whitby to Pickering—that had brought Stephenson to the coast, and it must have seemed small beer to him after his triumphs with the Stockton & Darlington and Liverpool & Manchester railways. Even the building of this line had, with true Yorkshire caution, involved more than 40 years of discussion. In 1793 a canal was proposed from Ruswarp to Pickering by way of Grosmont, Beckhole and Newtondale at an estimated cost of over £60,000. This scheme was not completely abandoned until 1831, but five years earlier a railway running along the same route from Whitby to Pickering was first mooted. Its supporters were influenced by the impending renewal of the Act for the turnpike between the two towns and the success of the Stockton & Darlington line for which Whitby folk had subscribed £8,500. A further development occurred in 1830 when John Hugill, liberty bailiff, published a 70-page pamphlet urging the local populace to shake off its despondent lethargy and form a company to prospect for coal in the district. If the search was successful a railway could then be built from Whitby through Pickering to Malton.

His proposals were somewhat nullified by the efforts of rival factions who advocated a line up Eskdale to link up with the Stockton & Darlington. Thomas Storey, engineer of this company, was asked to make a survey of this route, and gave his report to a meeting of interested parties held in Whitby on March 2nd, 1831. A further meeting at the *Angel Inn,* Whitby, on May 6th saw the formation of a provisional committee which cast considerable doubt on Storey's report—doubt which was intensified when he "modified" his estimate from £120,000 to £226,000! The Eskdale route fell further into disfavour in December 1831 when "A Townsman" published a pamphlet *Thoughts on a Railway from Whitby into the Interior* recommending a line to Pickering with a branch to Lealholme Bridge in preference to the Stockton route.

The committee ultimately resolved to ask George Stephenson for his comments on building "a line of simplest construction for the employment of animal power." In a report dated July 5th, 1832, Stephenson came down firmly against the Stockton scheme, claiming it would involve a climb of over 600 feet and would offer little effective competition against the existing sea route via Middlesbrough. But "Old George" was quite impressed with the idea of a line to Pickering, declaring somewhat optimistically that it would "amply remunerate the proprietors for the money invested". He argued that the route would cost about £2,000 per mile, but traffic in coal shipped from County Durham for transit to Pickering and the Vale of Ryedale would be worth about £6,000 a year. A further £7,200 per annum would be recouped if, as a counterbalancing working, the railway was used to carry lime for reclamation of the "barren tract" of the North York Moors lying alongside the track. The line would also improve the trade of Whitby harbour and enable Baltic and American timber, groceries, drugs, fish and other commodities imported into Whitby to reach Pickering and neighbouring towns for a considerably lower cost. In addition it would facilitate the transport of freestone from Eskdale and hardwoods and agricultural produce from the Pickering area, while the cost of delivering whinstone from Egton Bridge and Goathland to London would be greatly reduced.

This balanced and quietly optimistic report was received with "great satisfaction" at a meeting at the *Angel Inn* on September 12th, 1832. A share list was opened and within the space of a few weeks £30,000 had been subscribed. Stephenson had estimated that the gross receipts would be almost £13,000 per annum but the promoters, perhaps fearing miscalculations on Storey's scale, asked for a second estimate based on local knowledge. This was supplied by William Thompson of Whitby in a pamphlet *The Whitby & Pickering Railway: Its probable Traffic and Revenue* which put the gross receipts at almost £9,000 and the net receipts at £6,000—sufficient to yield a dividend of $7\frac{1}{2}$ per cent. These figures were contested in yet another pamphlet, this time written by "A Looker-On" from Pickering who with some foresight prophesied an annual deficiency of at least £175.

In the meantime the supporters had felt sufficiently confident to apply for an Act of Parliament which was obtained without opposition on May 6th, 1833. It contained several noteworthy features, including provision for the use of L-shaped plate rails if desired and an interesting list of tolls. Materials for the repair of roads were to be charged twopence per ton per mile; coal, lime, iron, bricks, potatoes and kelp, threepence; corn, flour, coke, manufactured iron, steel, timber and hay, fourpence; malt, meat, groceries, wool, fruit and vegetables, fivepence; and all other items, sixpence. Passengers were to pay twopence per mile, and an extra charge of one shilling per ton was to be made for all goods taken up—but not down—the incline. In fact the lawyers must have had a field day with this early piece of railway legislation for one section of the Act permitted the use of locomotives while another expressly forbade it!

Detailed surveying of the route now went ahead. From a terminus at Whitby, symbolically on the site of a former shipyard, it crossed the river Esk no less than nine times before Grosmont to enter the valley of the Murk Esk by means of a tunnel 120 yards in length. Beyond Beckhole the original intention was to take the line past Mallyan Spout and Wheel-

George Hudson 1800-1871 (above) had a strong affection for the Whitby and Pickering Railway, and was instrumental in connecting the line to the national rail network in the mid-1840s. His fall from power delayed Whitby's growth as a holiday resort (British Rail Eastern Region—detail from the portrait by Francis Grant which hangs in York Mansion House).

George Stephenson 1781-1848 (right) met Hudson in Whitby in 1834, and the two men struck up a lasting friendship. At the time the older George was superintending the construction of the railway to Pickering which he had laid out "for the employment of animal power" (National Portrait Gallery).

The Two Georges

dale Lodge before heading south by a long tunnel, but this approach was abandoned in favour of a rope-worked incline to Goathland. A summit level of over 500 feet was reached at Fen Bog near the entrance to the Ice Age gorge of Newtondale which was followed throughout its sinewy length to Pickering.

The initial contract for the section from Bog Hall to Sleights was let in August 1833, and the first sod cut on September 10th at Bog Hall by Robert Campion who had been appointed chairman of the company. Construction proceeded at what was a rapid rate considering the difficult terrain and the total lack of mechanical aids. One of the major works was the diversion of the Esk at Larpool Flat between Whitby and Ruswarp to save the expense of constructing two swing bridges. River crossings upstream from this point were made of Baltic fir, the first and longest being at Ruswarp. Henry Belcher gives some interesting details in his book on the line published in 1836: "It is 312 feet in length, being carried across the river in a diagonal direction, and divided into five portions of 62 feet span each—the frame work of the whole being supported upon four rows of piles 14 inches square, (placed obliquely so as to offer the least possible resistance to the natural and tidal currents of the river), and firmly strapped together by iron bands. The expense of this bridge, including the masonry, extras and cornices was £1,575." South of this point difficulties were created by boggy ground which caused embankments to subside, and by two cuttings through hard alum rock.

At Grosmont the tunnel was made with attractive castellated entrances to dimension 14 feet high and 10 feet wide. Beyond this point another major engineering work was the inclined plane between Beckhole and Goathland, while special problems were posed at the summit by the 20 feet deep Fen Bog. The difficulties were only overcome by "pile-driving" large balks of Baltic fir with hammers which were reputedly 14-lbs in weight. Sheaves of heather bound in sheep skins, whole trees and hurdles covered with cut moss were sacrificed to the bog in order to secure a firm foundation. Similar challenges had to be met in Newtondale, which Belcher described as "presenting the whole way a succession of the most difficult ground over which a railway has ever yet been attempted to be made. In fact, the whole of this length had to be formed over broken or boggy ground—in the course of moorland streams —through heaps of stones and earth that had subsided from the neighbouring cliffs and hills." During the construction a building in Newtondale known as Carter's Cottage temporarily became an inn to cater for thirsty navvies.

The track was laid with fish-bellied rails 15 feet in length weighing 40-lbs to the yard and resting in chairs fixed to massive stone blocks 24 inches square of at least 200-lbs weight. A curious feature, which has never been satisfactorily explained, was that the blocks were not laid at right-angles to the rails but diagonally. Stephenson's estimate of £2,000 per miles was left far behind as constructional difficulties were surmounted and the price of iron rose alarmingly; the line was ultimately to cost £105,600 or £4,400 per mile.

By May 15th, 1835, the works from Whitby to Whinstone Dyke on the south side of Grosmont tunnel were sufficiently completed to enable the directors to make a trial trip in the first-class carriage *Premier,* a vehicle which apart from flanged wheels made no concessions to evolution from the stage-coach. On June 8th it began to run regularly—except of course on the sabbath—between Whitby and the *Tunnel Inn* at Grosmont (or Growmond as it was then known), the fares being 1s. outside and 1s. 3d. inside. During the first three months it conveyed more than 6,000 folk, making two trips each way from Monday to Friday and three on Saturdays. From July 18th it was joined by a second-class coach which provided a service for market people for a fare of sixpence. With commendable enterprise in a period when tourism was scarcely conceived the company announced that the coaches would be available for hire by parties, and for a fare of 6d. per person it would be possible to go as far as Beckhole by engaging an extra coach. The line was thus the third in Yorkshire to convey passengers, being preceded by the Middlesbrough extension of the Stockton & Darlington Railway (opened December 27th, 1830) and the Leeds & Selby Railway (September 22nd, 1834). On the freight side some 10,000 tons of stone traffic was carried in the first 12 months from mid-1835; this came from the quarries of the Whitby Stone Company at Lease Rigg near Grosmont and was let down to the railway by a self-acting inclined plane. From Whitby it was shipped to London.

A coach also ran locally between Pickering and Raindale and in addition there was probably some through goods traffic prior to the formal opening of the complete line on May 26th, 1836. This day was one of the most colourful occasions in Whitby's history. The town's church bells began to peal at dawn and by 7.30 a.m. a huge crowd had assembled outside the *Angel Inn,* from where a procession to the station was led by the Whitby Brass Band. Passengers took their seats in carriages decorated with banners bearing the crest of the railway company, while the horses were summoned by the ringing of a bell. Each coachman and guard had a green card placed in his hat showing the coach to which he belonged. The bell was again rung for the horses to be attached to the carriages and the procession-on-wheels set off at a brisk pace, speed being regulated by the guards' flags. A white flag meant "go on", red "go slow" and blue "stop"—red had not yet become synonymous with danger. Thomas Clark, the first treasurer of the railway, commented: "Every part of the line where the public could have access to it, or where a view of the railway could be obtained, was crowded with spectators to witness the departure of the carriages: many flags were exhibited, and the most hearty cheers were given and returned by the bystanders and passengers in the coaches".

After a stop at the *Tunnel Inn,* the passengers reached Beckhole (then Beck Holes) where some anxiety was expressed about the ascent of the incline. But the contemporary account noted: "On the signal being given three carriages loaded with passengers glided up the steep ascent with a pleasing, rapid, and easy pace; and both on going and returning many were heard to declare that the ascending and descending of the incline so far from being in any way disagreeable, was certainly as pleasant as any other part of the day's journey. The other carriages followed in succession, and the band during the time played several enlivening airs to the manifest delight of a large assemblage of country people collected about the top of the inclined plane and who with colours flying and firing of guns welcomed the visitors".

At the summit of the line the horses were detached and the carriages coupled together before running down Newtondale by gravity at speeds touching 30 miles an hour. Fresh horses were attached when the coaches came to rest on the more level stretch of line at Blansby Park, four miles from Pickering. Arrival at this ancient market town was $1\frac{1}{4}$ hours late owing to the coach *Lady Hilda* having to be abandoned after three derailments. But the crowd of 7,000 people, assembled from points as far away as Scarborough and York, showed no signs of impatience and cheered "with one untied voice" as the carriages came into sight. Cannon were fired at intervals while five bands added to the cacophany of sound. A procession 300 strong left the station for the *Black Swan Inn* where "the party sat down to a most excellent dejeuner à la fourchette for which during the preceding fortnight most formidable preparations in the way of good eatables had been made". The return to Whitby was a similar gala event, and "those who delight in quickly passing through the air were gratified in being carried at the rate of 20 miles an hour". The port was regained at 5.0 p.m., and then 70 guests adjourned to the *Angel Inn* for a dinner which did not break up until 2.0 a.m. It had truly been a great day out.

The operating peculiarities which intrigued the first passengers have done much to account for the extraordinary present-day interest in a line only 24 miles long. An outstanding feature was the incline, 1,500 yards in length with a maximum gradient of 1 in 10 and resembling a stately avenue in the way it cut through a wood. Ascending coaches were hauled up in $4\frac{1}{2}$ minutes by being attached at Beckhole to a $5\frac{3}{4}$ inches thick hemp rope wound round a 10 feet diameter horizontal revolving drum at Bank Top (or Incline Top) station near Goathland (then Goadland). It took some time for trains to be reassembled at the top and in winter many passengers kept themselves warm by dashing up to the village inn for a pint; in summer the landlord obliged by erecting a beer tent alongside the railway. Descending power was provided by a four-ton water tank on wheels which was topped up with water from two reservoirs near the station; at Beckhole the water was emptied into the Murk Esk while a white flag or handkerchief was hung out so that a nearby farmer could have his team of horses in readiness to take the tank back to the top. This rather crude system was later replaced by a stationary steam engine, a van fitted with brake blocks pressing on the rails then being attached to each train. Even this did not prevent Charles Dickens commenting that he had travelled on a "quaint old railway along part of which passengers are hauled by a rope".

On the journey from Whitby one set of horses worked as far as Beckhole and then another set from Bank Top to the summit at Fen Bog. A further relay took the coaches on to Raindale Posting House near Levisham (then Leavisham), although on the steepest part of the descending gradient it became customary to couple two coaches together and let them proceed by their own momentum. Horses were again used for the approach to Pickering. On the return journey two horses were required to draw each coach over the severe gradients between Raindale Mill and the summit, but gravity was used from Beckhole to Grosmont. During gravity runs the horses earned a free ride for their uphill efforts by being placed in dandy carts coupled to the carriages.

There were normally two trains each way per day and it took almost $2\frac{1}{2}$ hours to make the through journey from

One Horse-Power Days

Celebrations to mark the opening of the Whitby and Pickering Railway included the publication of a book extolling the virtues of the surrounding scenery. It contained several superb steel engravings by George Dodgson 1811-1880, a noted water colourist who was at one time apprenticed to George Stephenson and prepared the plans for the line. The three engravings reproduced here are:- Opposite page, upper: Grosmont (then Growmond) showing the original bridge over the Murk Esk and the castellated horse tunnel. Opposite, lower: A first-class carriage enters the then remote Newtondale. Above: Hailing the coach during stormy weather in Newtondale.

Whitby to Pickering, but this was a great improvement on the hilly coach road via Saltergate which until the motoring age became so grass grown as to scarcely show up from the surrounding heather. The first-class carriages—*Premier* and *Lady Hilda* in bright yellow and *Transit* in green—each held six inside passengers, four in front outside, four behind outside and as many as could be squeezed on top. They were light vehicles weighing only four tons and costing £280. There were steps to the top deck, the driver sitting in a dickey placed at the front with a footboard beneath and the brake lever within convenient reach. Initially the fares were: first class, inside, 5s; first class, outside, 5s; second class 3s. A month after opening these figures were reduced to 3s. 6d., 3s. and 2s. 6d. The first tickets were printed by Messrs. Horne and Richardson of Whitby, and were on coloured paper which had to be filled in by the booking clerk with the number of the coach and seat, the date and time and the destination. The same details were entered on a counterfoil and the ticket then torn out of its book. Printed on the tickets were the requests "When seated be pleased to hold this ticket in your hand till called for" and "Notice—no gratuity allowed to be taken by any Guard, Porter or other Servant of the Company". Loss of tickets and tipping were clearly already firmly established.

The first gentleman's carriage to pass over the railway was hauled up the line on a truck on September 29th, 1836, with its 86-year-old owner and his two daughters inside. The octogenarian, an Essex worthy, was highly delighted with the novel method of travel. A further novelty was the sponsoring by the company of some of the first railway excursions on record on August 7th and 8th, 1839. The occasion was a bazaar held at Grosmont to raise money to build St. Matthew's Church, and the normal fares from Whitby (9d.) and Pickering (2s. 3d.) were reduced to 6d. and 1s. 6d. respectively. Coaches were run from Whitby every hour and from Pickering as often as required, the company making the announcement: "The (first) train will leave at 5 a.m. and parties will have to be wide awake or they will suffer disappointment. Promptitude on the part of the Railway Company calls for the same from passengers." One John Watkins was inspired to write a ballad, *The Tunnel Bazaar,* part of which ran:

> *A church it is said will be built at the tunnel,*
> *With steeple no doubt that will serve as a funnel,*
> *Through which "spirit" fumes will ascend on high*
> *Like smoke through a chimney in clouds to the sky.*

The venture evidently achieved the desired effect for a little over a year later—on September 16th, 1840—special trains were run for the laying of the foundation stone of the church.

Another peculiarity was the company's bye-laws which stipulated a fine of £5 for any person using out-of-gauge wagons on the line, and a penalty of £2 if wagons were used on the railway between two hours after sunset and one hour before sunrise. But although the operation of the line did in some respects verge on the comic, its achievements were considerable. Whitby harbour commissioners were compelled by the increased trade to make improvements to the port, while a steam packet company was formed to import goods from Hull and Newcastle for forwarding on the railway. Pickering felt the effects of the transport revolution when cargoes of goods from London began to reach the town in three days. Limestone was conveyed from Pickering to four large kilns erected at Grosmont, and two companies were established to bring sea borne coal from Whitby to Pickering. In 1838 both a brick and tile works and a bone crushing and saw mill came into operation at Ruswarp. Apart from Lease Rigg, stone also came from other quarries in the Goathland area and was drawn to either Bank Top or Beckhole stations by a team of oxen. This stone is said to have been used in the construction of such famous London buildings as Covent Garden and Somerset House. The railway also led to the birth of the great Cleveland iron industry for in 1836 a partner of the Tyne Iron Company recognised an outcrop of ironstone at Grosmont, the convenient access to a port enabling this to be worked by the Whitby Stone Company. Three years later the Wylam Iron Company began operations in the area, and these were much expanded when taken over by the world-famous firm of Bolckow, Vaughan & Co. of Middlesbrough. For many years all ironstone mined in Cleveland came from Grosmont.

From the outset passenger traffic exceeded expectations, 3,903 folk for instance being conveyed in July 1836 and no less than 4,200 the following month. In six months in 1837 the total number of passengers travelling over the line increased 8,000 on the previous six months. But despite these seemingly rosy figures the railway was from the very start in financial difficulties, caused in part by the enormous discrepancy between the estimated and actual cost of construction. A meeting held towards the end of 1836 was told the company was in debt to the tune of £13,000, and on May 5th, 1837, an Act had to be obtained to raise £30,000 additional capital.

It was also later calculated that to take only 120 tons of ironstone from Grosmont to Whitby required 20 horses under the charge of ten men, hardly an economic prospect. Yet for another eight years the Whitby & Pickering Railway remained in a state of glorious isolation, the coaches rattling up and down the track at a pace unruffled by internal difficulties or outside events. As early as 1834 Stephenson had surveyed two lines from Pickering to York—one via Malton and the other through Easingwold—but it was not until 1845 that the line was at last connected with the rapidly expanding national railway network. Even then change was not immediate for two years later Bradshaw's timetable still noted: "Whitby Branch—By Horse Power. From Pickering to Whitby at 9.0 a.m. and 2.0 p.m. From Whitby to Pickering at 7.0 a.m. and 1.30 p.m." The railway had ceased to make concessions to progress.

Old and new tunnels at Grosmont (John M. Boyes).

A Century
of Development

G EORGE HUDSON became greatly and perhaps genuinely concerned that the Whitby and Pickering Railway was being left out on a limb, and for this reason was ceasing to be a financial success. He was chairman of the York & North Midland Railway, and in 1840 cajoled the shareholders of the company to release £500 of the profits to survey lines from York to Scarborough and Pickering. The Railway King was almost right when he felt this would enable Scarborough to become "the Brighton of the North", but perhaps the link to Pickering was of more personal significance to him for it would put an end to the isolation of his favourite town of Whitby. Also, although not a soul must know, would it not help him to achieve his ambition of becoming Member of Parliament for the port?

The warm relationship between Hudson and Whitby was a mutual one. Local fisherfolk admired him for the way he dropped all arrogant pretensions when in their midst. And they were captivated when the Railway King came face to face with one Gawan Pierson, King of Goathland, and Thomas Toddles, King of Staithes. The three pseudo monarchs thought it was a huge joke as they walked in mock parade solemnly exchanging salutes. But it needed more than pretence pageantry to solve the ills of the Whitby and Pickering line. Hudson declared that the best hope in rejuvenating the railway lay in turning Whitby into a holiday resort, and he set about this task with his usual vigour. West Cliff fields were purchased and the Whitby Building Company formed to facilitate their development; rows of terraced boarding houses were laid out in an area where George Street and Hudson Street remain to this day, while the *Royal Hotel* went up on a site opposite the Abbey. A road called Khyber Pass was constructed to afford easier access to the shore.

In the meantime the directors of the Whitby and Pickering Railway, after initially considering amalgamation with the Stockton & Darlington company, plumped for the York & North Midland when it obtained its Act for lines to Scarborough and Pickering on July 4th, 1844. The purchase price was agreed at £80,000—some £25,000 less than the cost of construction but by this time the affairs of the line seem to have reached an all-time low. During a nine month period it achieved the doubtful distinction of paying a mere £1 19s. 6¾d. in passenger duty to the Government, the lowest figure of any railway in the country and representing an income of only £1 per week from passenger travel. Matters began to improve after an Act was obtained on June 30th, 1845, authorising the York & North Midland to purchase the line and rebuild it for locomotive haulage.

Heavier rails were laid and the line doubled, a stone bridge built at Grosmont and five iron bridges constructed across the Esk, a new and larger tunnel excavated at Grosmont, deviations made to eliminate the sharper curves, new stations laid out at Whitby and Pickering, permanent buildings erected at the intermediate stations, and the perilous hemp rope on the incline replaced by wire. From July 7th, 1845, steam locomotives began to appear at the extreme southern end of the line with the opening of the railway from York to Scarborough and its branch from Rillington to Pickering. By August 1846 steam had penetrated as far as Raindale, but it was July 1st, 1847, before the first locomotive, a 2-2-0, entered Whitby. Engine sheds were built at Beckhole because the incline made through working impossible.

Hudson's dream of turning Whitby into a flourishing resort collapsed when the exposure of his dubious financial practices created a public outcry in the late 1840s. Yet the town—and the railway—entered a new lease of life through a mere whim of fashion. Jet, which had been worked in the locality since the Bronze Age, suddenly lept into popularity when Queen Victoria selected it for mourning. By 1850 the town boasted over 50 jet workshops, and this number gradually climbed to a peak figure of 200 employing 1,500 men. The fortunes of the line were also favoured by extension of quarrying operations in the Goathland area, but much more important was the growth of the Cleveland iron industry. Ironworks were built at Beckhole in 1859 along with houses for 180 workmen, but owing to a series of disasters—including the collapse of both the mine and a furnace—production ceased only two years later. More successful were the Grosmont Ironworks which

Nineteenth century Whitby. Enlargement of part of a photograph taken by Frank Sutcliffe from Larpool, half a mile from Town station. It shows both railway and harbour bustling with activity at a time when the local jet industry was still flourishing.

opened about 1863 and remained in blast until 1891; in their heyday they provided work for four standard gauge locomotives including a vertical-boilered engine.

Even when rebuilt the railway still retained some very sharp curves. It was once a common quip that the driver and guard of a train used to shake each other by the hand at certain points of the journey, while churns filled with milk at Whitby were reputed to contain butter when they arrived at Pickering! The curves at Fen Bog were the scene of a derailment on August 6th, 1859, caused by the hot sun buckling the track; an entire train plunged into the swamp and the driver and fireman had to be extricated by passengers from what could have been a very murky end. This was the first of three serious accidents which plagued the line at this period. On October 12th, 1861, the rope on the incline broke when a mineral train was being hauled up to Bank Top—the brakes-man jumped for his life but the wagons careered down the gradient at great speed crashing into a goods train which had just arrived from Whitby. Happily there were no fatal injuries.

Worse was to come on February 10th, 1864. The last passenger train into Whitby had been lowered about 150 yards down the incline when the rope snapped. It was a frosty night and, although Guard Joseph Sedman bravely stuck to his van in an effort to check the speed of the train, the rails were too icy for the brakes to have any effect. The coaches overturned at the bottom killing two commercial travellers and injuring 13 other people. At a subsequent Board of Trade inquiry it was stated the rope was defective through having been run over by a train, and was due to have been taken out of service the day after the disaster. The inquest jury brought in a rider that the rope was definitely unfit for use, and expressed surprise that it was not regularly examined by a superior officer. As a result of the accident a purse of 60 guineas was awarded to the guard as a token of his bravery, while a stronger rope was installed and telegraphic communication instituted between the upper and lower ends of the incline.

But, ironically, measures were in hand at the time of both these runaways to eliminate what had become a dangerous bottleneck as well as a source of more odorous complications, such as the occasion when a train laden with herrings got out of control and left a fish-like smell hanging over the surrounding area for weeks. On July 11th, 1861, the North Eastern Railway (formed in 1854 by an amalgamation of the York & North Midland and three other companies) had obtained an Act to build a deviation line $4\frac{1}{2}$ miles long from a point south of the tunnel at Grosmont to link up with the original course near Fen Bog. It was an extremely difficult piece of construction, costing no less than £50,000. Two farmsteads had to be completely demolished and replaced on a different site, while it was necessary to divert and build a new bridge for the road from Green End to Beckhole. Seven bridges had to be constructed over the river Murk Esk, including one impressive structure on twin stone pillars and another with a skew arch crossing over an existing footbridge as well as the water. Most taxing of all was a half mile long cutting where huge boulders had to be blasted away—and then rock falls became so frequent it was necessary for watchmen to patrol the line from 10.0 p.m. to 6.0 a.m.

These engineering problems meant that a tense 17 months

Scenes at Beckhole. Top: The Fell-locomotive destined for Brazil which in 1872 was tested on a special track laid on the course of the original incline from Beckhole to Goathland (collection of K. Hoole). Bottom: Arrival of the first autocar at the re-opened Beckhole station on July 1st, 1908; this summer-only service was withdrawn in 1914 (collection of Mrs. G. E. Deakin).

elapsed between the incline fatalities and the elimination of the bank by the opening of the 1 in 49 deviation on July 1st, 1865. With the abandonment of the halts at Beckhole and Bank Top, a station was built on the new line and took the name Goathland Mill from its proximity to the village water mill. Later the name was shortened to Goathland. It soon became a centre of industrial activity when the Duchy of Lancaster agreed to the construction of a tramway from the station to stone quarries on Silhowe, one of the highest points in the immediate area. The tramway was worked by a combination of horses and gravity, and after some 30 years quarrying was superseded by whinstone mining.

The introduction of through locomotive working to Whitby following the by-passing of the incline brought several developments in its wake. Edward Fletcher, the first locomotive engineer of the North Eastern Railway, designed a special class of engines to cope with the sharp curves and steep gradients on the line. They had unusually small coupled wheels only five feet in diameter and were of the 4-4-0 wheel arrangement; as most North Eastern engines at this time were "single" drivers or 2-4-0s they quickly acquired the nickname of "Whitby Bogies". Other locomotives were adapted to provide rear-end assistance from Grosmont to the summit and were fitted with a special coupling which enabled the banker to drop off at the top without stopping the train. When through carriages began to run between Kings Cross and Whitby in the summer months, these too were of a special design with only four wheels and were jocularly referred to as "Whitby bathing machines". Six-wheeled coaches were barred from the line and four-wheeled vehicles limited to a maximum wheelbase of 19 feet; bogie carriages did not appear until the turn of the century.

On the fringe of the Whitby-Pickering line a new curve was opened at Rillington on the same date as the deviation; it enabled cheap excursion trains to run through from Scarborough to Whitby but was closed as an economy measure on October 1st, 1866. More permanent lines were however completed which put an end to Whitby's long-felt insularity. The project for a railway up the Esk Valley which had first been mooted in the 1820s finally came to fruition on October 2nd, 1865, with the opening of a branch from Grosmont to Castleton where it linked up with lines already in existence to Middlesbrough via Great Ayton and to Picton between Northallerton and Stockton. In the same year Whitby station was enlarged and improved. A decade later Pickering became

Sentinel steam railcars were introduced on the line in 1927. One is seen here passing Darnholm—one of the most attractive points on the route—on a trip-working between Whitby and Goathland (C. M. Doncaster).

a junction when a branch was opened on April 1st, 1875, to Kirkby Moorside; here it joined an earlier line to Gilling and Pilmoor on the East Coast route. Pickering further increased in importance when the branch to Seamer came into operation on May 1st, 1882. The final development was the construction of a line along the coast; the section from Whitby to Loftus (where a connection was made with tracks to Saltburn and Middlesbrough) was brought into use on December 3rd, 1883, while July 16th, 1885, saw traffic using the rails from Scarborough to West Cliff, Whitby.

Surprisingly developments also occurred on the abandoned stretch of line between Grosmont and Fen Bog. The old incline was selected for trials when Manning, Wardle & Co. of Boyne Engine Works, Leeds, built a Fell-locomotive for an extension of the coffee-carrying Cantagallo Railway between Caxoeira and Nova Friburgo in the province of Rio de Janeiro, Brazil. Track was laid to a gauge of 3ft. 7ins., the gradient steepened and two sharp curves introduced with a radius of 1 in 87. A double-headed centre rail was placed edgewise to provide uphill momentum when gripped by the four horizontal friction wheels on the locomotive. On May 6th, 1872, the engine reached Goathland after a difficult journey from Leeds owing to limited clearances. Official trials took place on June 21st and 22nd when 30 intrepid passengers and four loaded wagons were successfully hauled up the 750-yard long gradient in 3½ minutes, thus producing the comment that the old incline need never have been abandoned! The feat created a great deal of excitement in the locality, and it was a sad July 13th when this short piece of South American railway history set on the North York Moors came to an end with the departure of the locomotive for Brazil.

A further revival on this section occurred during the first golden flush of tourism in the Edwardian years. The rails had been left in place from Deviation Junction near Grosmont to the foot of the incline, and it was decided to use them for a summer-only autocar and railcar service from Whitby. Temporary buildings were erected to enable the former Beck Holes station to reopen as Beckhole on July 1st, 1908, and the service proved quite popular until the outbreak of war caused it to be withdrawn on September 21st, 1914, never to be resumed. The other casualty of the war was the four mile stretch of line between Pickering New Bridge and Levisham which was singled with the object of supplying track for use in France. It was a noble idea, but alas the ship carrying the rails was torpedoed and they now lie at the bottom of the English Channel.

In the years after the first world war the significant feature of the Whitby-Pickering railway was that so little changed. Grouping in 1923 brought few drastic alterations, although new London & North Eastern Railway "Hunt" classes began to displace ex-N.E.R. types on some passenger workings. Similarly on the freight side ex-Hull & Barnsley Railway 0-6-0s were drafted to Whitby and Pickering sheds but were not popular. An interesting experiment began in 1927 when Sentinel steam railcars started to work over the line, some on trial and others in regular service including trip workings from Whitby Town to West Cliff and to Goathland. They were withdrawn by 1937.

Undoubtedly the most important change was Whitby's increasing prominence as a tourist resort, which enabled the town to recover from a decline caused by the collapse of the jet industry during changing moods of fashion at the beginning of the 20th century. Summer excursion trains became an increasing factor in the working of the line and particularly so Sunday scenic excursions. These were run from various West Riding centres and usually worked outward via Pickering to arrive at Whitby in time for a pause for lunch. The journey continued along the coast to Scarborough where tea was taken, and then the return home made through Seamer and Malton. They were eight-coach trains packed with passengers revelling in a good day out, and made a brave sight when piloted up Newtondale by a 4-6-2 tank from Malton to the summit. Smiling faces jammed the carriage windows as the smell of the moors gave way to the tang of the sea. Even when it was a case of home at last one could always look forward to next year and the year after that, for would not the railway always be running?

Post-1847 engraving of railway at Grosmont (Harold D. Bowtell).

Glimpses of a Golden Age

F OR more than a hundred years the steep gradients, sharp curves and superb setting of the Whitby and Pickering line have provided ideal material for the railway photographer. Among the first-known illustrations showing the route are studies by Frank M. Sutcliffe of Whitby, the early and now world-famous exponent of camera art. His pioneer work laid the foundations for hundreds of views taken down the years showing the railway in all its aspects—trains panting uphill, new forms of motive power, shed scenes, goods traffic, Sunday excursions, engineering features, station staff. Only in 1959 with the onset of dieselisation did the line begin to lose some of its perennial camera appeal, and now many of the photographs of earlier years form a nostalgic record of a bygone era. The following nine pages of illustrations depict the railway in the full glory of its golden age.

Opposite: Contrasts in motive power. Top: One of the "Whitby Bogies" specially designed by Edward Fletcher to cope with the sharp curves and steep gradients on the line. No. 1809, originally No. 496, was built by Robert Stephenson & Co. in 1865, rebuilt as shown in 1889 and scrapped in 1893 (British Rail Eastern Region). Bottom: The lady in shorts belies the date! In fact it is as early as August 1927, and the Sentinel steam railcar "Hark Forward" is pausing at Goathland on a trial run from Whitby (W. H. Tate).

Three Studies by Frank Sutcliffe:

Whitby forms the subject of what is probably the finest 19th century photographic portrayal of a town in all its aspects. It is the work of Frank M. Sutcliffe 1853-1941, internationally famous for his glass-plate studies of local fisherfolk and sailing ships. Numerous railway subjects are included in his 1,500 photographs of the Whitby area, and among them are:- Opposite page, top: A remarkable shot taken in the early 1880s showing Esk Viaduct in its initial stages of construction; a temporary siding crosses the river to the Whitby and Pickering railway. Opposite, bottom: It is difficult today to imagine that Grosmont was ever like this, for all traces of the ironworks, which were in blast from about 1863 to 1891, have disappeared. This view was taken about 1889 and shows a Fletcher locomotive in the station. Above: Variety in moustaches, beards and costume is clearly evident in this 1888 study of Whitby Town's station staff.

Scenes from the 1930s:- Opposite page: Ex-Hull & Barnsley Railway 0-6-0s drafted to the line during this period, both photographed near Levisham. This page, top: A delightful view of one of the noted Sunday scenic excursions near Levisham in 1935. Bottom: A 4-6-2 tank passes Darnholm on the climb to Goathland (this page, lower: C. M. Doncaster; remainder L & GRP).

Steam in Full Cry:

The Whitby and Pickering Railway is personified in this stirring study of the morning Whitby-Leeds train being banked out of Grosmont. Steam everywhere, a begrimed leading engine and the motley collection of rolling stock combine to form an unforgettable picture of a bygone age. It was taken by J. W. Armstrong in August 1939 only days before the outbreak of the second world war.

The Changing Years. Opposite page:- Three eras at Whitby locomotive sheds: Top: 1880 (L&GRP). Centre: 1920. Bottom: 1952 (both J. W. Armstrong). This page, top: A G5 leaves Levisham during early British Railways' days (collection of Cecil Ord). Bottom: Dieselisation in evidence at Whitby Town in May 1966 (Harold D. Bowtell).

Closure and Re-birth

THE second world war shattered for ever the calm complacency which for so long had hung over the affairs of the Whitby and Pickering line. Excursion workings, scenic rail tours and through coaches to and from London all made their re-appearance in the summer months, but the upsurge in private motoring meant that the railway never regained its monopolistic self-assurance. Nationalisation brought a further increase in the variety of locomotive types, ex-London Midland & Scottish Railway 2-6-2 and 2-6-4 tanks being allocated to Whitby shed and class 5MT 4-6-0s making regular appearances on through trains from the West Riding. Interesting operating features of this period included the Monday market day special from Pickering to Summit signal box which enabled womenfolk living miles from the nearest road to maintain contact with the outside world. The working time-table noted that the train stopped "at Farworth, Roundale, Bridge No. 60 and Newton Dale to set down platelayers' wives". Railway workers living at these lonely places invented their own way of posting letters. A sapling willow or hazel was bent to the shape of a bow into which a slit was cut to affix the envelopes, and the bow then held up for one of the engine crew to slip his arm through. Isolation was also counteracted by the fortnightly special conveying coal and provisions to the roadless hamlet of Esk Valley between Grosmont and the abandoned terminus at Beckhole. When closure of this branch south of Deviation Junction became inevitable owing to the poor state of the track, the residents of the hamlet clubbed together to raise the necessary finance for a new North Riding County Council road. It was opened on October 1st, 1951, and the old route between Grosmont and Fen Bog soon became grass grown for its entire length.

The 1950s saw the beginning of the closures which were to eliminate most of the picturesque branch lines in the North York Moors area. January 31st, 1953, not only brought one of the worst storms ever to hit Britain but also the end of Pickering's seven decades as a junction. It was on this wild night that the last train chugged its way between Pickering and York via Kirkby Moorside and Gilling—already passenger services on the Pickering-Seamer-Scarborough route had been withdrawn on June 5th, 1950. A bigger blow to local prestige came on May 5th, 1958, with the shut-down of the coast line from Whitby to Loftus. New prosperity seemed to be at hand when multiple unit diesels were introduced on the remaining routes into Whitby in 1958 and 1959, (causing the closure of Whitby shed on April 6th, 1959) but although they were packed to capacity at summer week-ends there were all too many empty seats mid-week and mid-winter. It was not a situation to delight economists trying to halt British Railways mounting deficit. The great shock came with the publication of the Beeching Plan which proposed to turn the clock back almost 130 years to Georgian times and make Whitby again a railwayless town. The resulting furore was such it was decided to retain the route to Middlesbrough via Grosmont and Battersby, but on March 8th, 1965, harsh economics gained a shallow victory over social necessity when closure took place of both the Whitby-Scarborough line and the section of the Whitby and Pickering railway south of Grosmont.

British Railways' claim that the Pickering line had been losing £50,000 a year was disputed locally, several councils in the area getting together in an attempt to re-open the route by subsidising its operations. Then these last-ditch moves suddenly collapsed and it seemed the end. But rather than give up the fight completely a few local people held a meeting on June 3rd, 1967, the upshot being the formation of the North Yorkshire Moors Railway Preservation Society. Its members were convinced that if sufficient voluntary help was forthcoming the line could be made a viable proposition. After all, it was one of the most historic railways in the North running through a National Park among superb surroundings and by its proximity to coastal resorts having a high traffic potential. It also fulfilled a definite social need for in the winter months the Goathland area was frequently cut off from the outside world by road and became totally dependent on the railway.

By September 1967 rumours were abroad that the tracks were about to be lifted, so members of the preservation society

hurriedly arranged a meeting with British Railways. The result was an undertaking that while purchase costs were being calculated the lines would be left in situ, but at the end of six months the situation would be reviewed "in the light of the society's progress". Meanwhile interest in saving the line was spreading fast, and when an open meeting was held at Goathland the parish hall was packed to overflowing. Villagers as well as railway enthusiasts from all parts of the country approved the formation of the North Yorkshire Moors Railway Company to place negotiations with British Railways on a proper footing.

A few months later it became apparent that acquisition of the entire railway from Grosmont to Pickering would cost in the region of £100,000. The sum was boosted to six figures because much of the line was heavily check-railed to protect the sharp curves, while the track was in very good condition and was considered by the Railways Board to be re-usable material. Clearly the raising of such a large amount was beyond the society's means, so plans were drawn up afresh. After protracted negotiations a purchase price of £40,000 was agreed for the $6\frac{3}{4}$ miles of track and railway property from Grosmont to Eller Beck near the summit of the line and the very reasonable sum of £2,500 for the remaining $11\frac{1}{4}$ miles

Re-awakening. Opposite: A cat lazing on weed-grown tracks at Grosmont symbolises the period of closure (David Joy). Above: Mass turn-out at Goathland on February 2nd, 1969, to see "Mirvale" become the first engine to run over the line since closure (John M. Boyes).

of track-bed on to Pickering. The deal included only a single line of rails, apart from passing loops, but did incorporate six cottages at Grosmont tunnel, three at Farworth, two at Levisham, and the stations at Grosmont (up platform only), Goathland and Levisham. At the time of writing there is still a chance of the track also being acquired from Eller Beck to Levisham, but in any event the possibility will always remain open of restoring the rails right through to Pickering at some future date. When achieved this ultimate aim will create the longest preserved standard gauge railway in the country. Furthermore there is little likelihood of the line losing its connection with British Railways at Grosmont for the scramble to exploit potash deposits in the area is virtually certain to give Whitby's sole surviving rail link a new lease of life.

The next major milestone in the process of restoration will be the granting of a Light Railway Transfer Order by the Ministry of Transport enabling a public passenger service to be operated. But in the meantime the process of deterioration and decay has been halted. Since November 10th, 1968, British Railways have allowed members of the Society access to the line for maintenance purposes, and week-end working parties and works trains have become a familiar sight. Unglamorous but essential tasks which have been accomplished include track-weeding, re-painting, repairs to fences and walls, cleaning of ditches and drains, lopping of overhanging bushes and removal of landslips.

Helping in this work has been an army of volunteers for the Society has managed to enroll its two thousandth member within two years of being founded—an amazing average of almost 200 members a month. People from all walks of life have rallied together with the common aim of seeing the line re-opened. The five local authorities concerned with the area have all become corporate members, while solicitors, barristers, plumbers, builders and tradesmen willingly give up their spare time to offer what help they can. Railwaymen of all grades and departments are among the keenest of supporters, and several schools are corporate members, the railway thus

The less glamorous tasks in running a railway. Left, top: A week-end working party restores a bridge parapet damaged by vandals. Bottom: Students of both sexes have made a round trip of 150 miles from Newcastle University to weed the track. Right: Mr. J. Brown, a B.R. permanent way inspector, provides professional supervision (David Joy).

providing valuable leisure activities for young people. Working parties come from a wide area and include students from the universities of Leeds, Hull and Newcastle; female students frequently help in weeding the track thus showing that the fair sex is not to be outdone when it comes to practical work on the line! Groups affiliated to the Society have been formed for Bridlington, London, the Midlands, North Teesside, Pickering, Tyneside and York, their members providing practical help and assisting in fund-raising. Methods of obtaining finance have ranged from the formation of a 200 Club to a sponsored walk along the line, and have included such diverse activities as garden parties, slide shows, whist drives, football competitions, snowball teas, coffee mornings and jumble sales. Yard lengths of track are being sold for £3 each.

The most outward sign of the railway's new lease of life has been the arrival of three steam locomotives, the first of them being delivered at Pickering by road on January 25th, 1969. It is *Mirvale,* a neat-looking 0-4-0 saddle tank built by Hudswell-Clarke of Leeds for the Mirvale Chemical Company, Mirfield, as recently as 1955. When the engine became redundant in 1968 it was bought by Mr. Raymond E. Dixon of Mollington, Cheshire, and offered to the North Yorkshire Moors Railway on permanent loan. February 2nd, 1969, was a red-letter day reminiscent of the line's original opening ceremony for it saw what was both the first engine working over the railway for almost four years and the preservation society's first train movement. Freshly fallen snow and brilliant sunshine provided a perfect background as *Mirvale* steamed out of Pickering and puffed slowly up Newtondale. Enthusiasts came from as far away as Leicester, and at Goathland an estimated crowd of 500 gathered to see life return to a line that had for so long lain dormant. Halts were made en route for the benefit of B.B.C. and other cameramen, but after a three hour journey the engine arrived at a Grosmont station almost lost beneath flags and a cheering crowd. *Mirvale* will be used for general and light duties.

Two more locomotives arrived at Pickering by road in March 1969. One is No. 3, a rare 0-4-0 well tank built by E. Borrows and Sons of St. Helens in 1898 for the Smelting Corporation, Ellesmere Port. About 1907 it was bought by the Wallsend Slipway and Engineering Company for shunting in their Tyneside shipyard, and somewhat spoilt in outline when converted to oil-firing in 1958. By June 1967 the locomotive had been lying semi-derelict for some months, so the

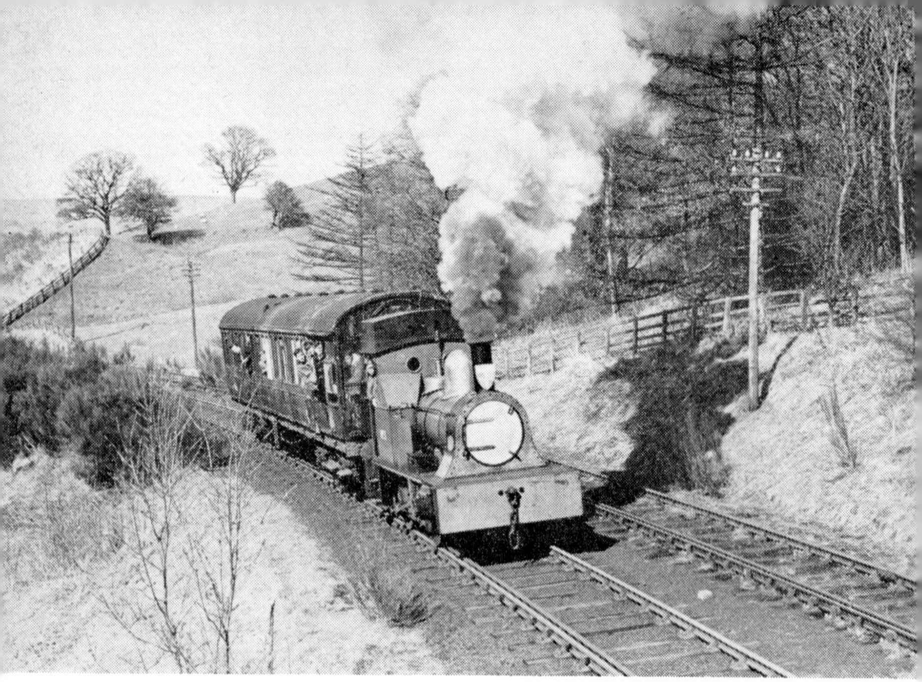

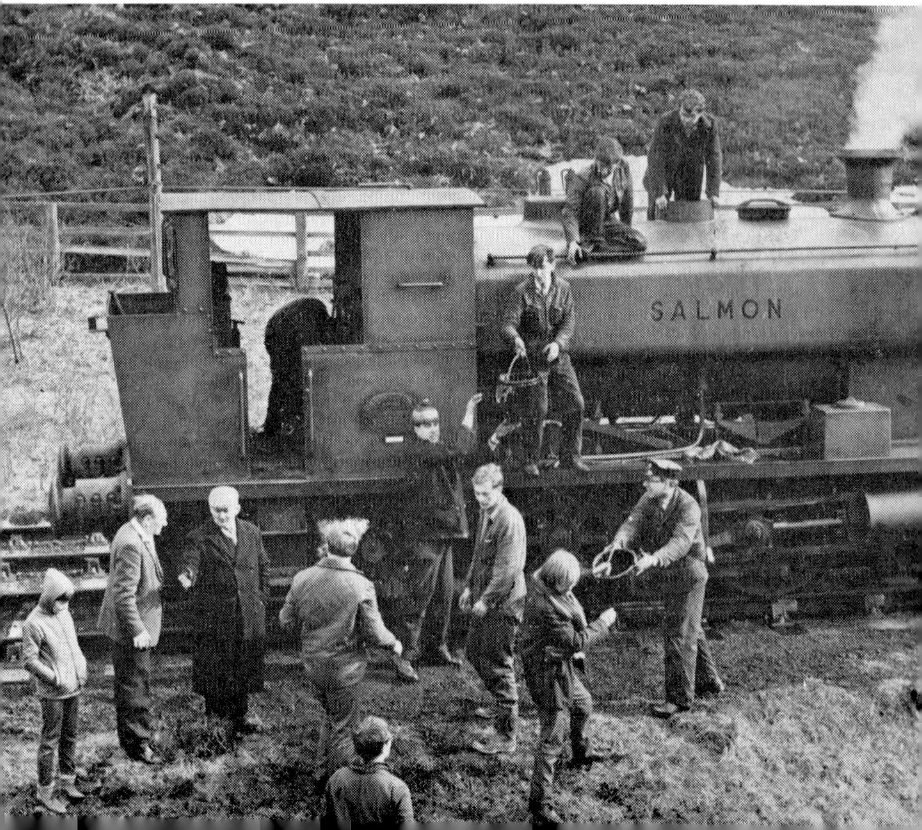
SALMON

Return of Steam:

The first three engines to be made available to the preservation society. Opposite page, top: A Borrows well-tank built in 1898 hauls the preserved Hull & Barnsley Railway coach past Green End Wood, near Beckhole, on April 27th, 1969—thus forming the first passenger train over the line since closure. Bottom: Crisis at Ellerbeck: "Salmon", an Andrew Barclay saddle tank, makes an emergency stop for unconventional bucket-chain refreshment during its journey from Pickering to Grosmont on March 30th, 1969. Above: "Mirvale", a Hudswell Clarke saddle tank, meets a rail-motor trolley at the summit when making its first run over the line on a snowy February 2nd, 1969 (John M. Boyes).

Newcastle University Railway Society obtained permission to undertake restoration work on it. No. 3 finally became redundant in October 1968, and the shipyard decided to present the engine to the University society as a gift in recognition of the hard work put in by members. The well tank received many more hours of attention before a small ceremony at Wallsend on March 17th preceded its departure by road low-loader. It too is on permanent loan.

Salmon, a rather severe 0-6-0 saddle tank, was built by Andrew Barclay of Kilmarnock in 1942 and spent most of its working life at Woolsthorpe iron ore quarry near Grantham. In 1961 it had a major overhaul and thus was in good condition when dieselisation came to the quarry in 1968. The engine was bought by Mr. P. D. Smith of Doncaster who, after encountering several snags, had it moved to Pickering by low-loader on March 28th. Two days later *Salmon* was steamed to haul No. 3 on an eventful journey to Grosmont. A halt had to be made before Levisham as the well tank was running a hot box—the penalty of years of virtual dis-use. Then a second unplanned stop was necessary to raise steam on the climb to the summit. Finally *Salmon* twice ran out of water, a crisis only remedied by the footplate crews forming a human chain to pass buckets from a nearby stream. It was a situation not without the comic elements so well portrayed in the film *The Titfield Thunderbolt.* Despite these early tribulations *Salmon* is now in excellent condition and has proved capable of hauling 100-ton loads up the 1 in 49 incline to Goathland.

It is expected that two ex-British Railways engines will soon be loaned to the North Yorkshire Moors Railway by the North Eastern Locomotive Preservation Group, which was formed in November 1966 and set out to save one of the last examples of both the J27 and Q6 classes. Both types of mineral engine had been working in the North East for over 50 years, and because of their simplicity and ruggedness of design became the last pre-grouping locomotives to be employed on British Railways. After 12 months of hard fund-raising J27 0-6-0 No. 65894 built in 1923 was purchased for £1,400 on December 1st, 1967. A fund was then launched to preserve the last remaining Q6 0-8-0 No. 63395 built in 1919, and by a remarkable achievement the full purchase price of £2,300 was raised in less than six months. The J27 has since been overhauled in the National Coal Board workshops at Philadelphia at a cost of £620. When the engines are fully restored it is hoped to move them from their present home to

Grosmont in steam via Middlesbrough, Battersby and the Esk Valley; they will be a big asset on the steep gradients in times of heavy summer traffic.

A less impressive but most essential traction unit already on the line is a 46-seat diesel railbus of the type used by British Railways in the late 1950s when attempting to make minor branch lines commercially viable. It was bought from the Scottish Region of B.R. for £450 and is intended to provide the basic passenger service for residents and tourists. The railbus has heating, remote-controlled sliding doors and retractable steps which will enable passengers to be picked up at stops other than stations. Two more utilitarian vehicles which perform yeoman service are a pair of railmotors— motorised trolleys used by gangers to move sleepers and other heavy equipment.

In the acquisition of passenger coaches much is being achieved by a close association with the Hull & Barnsley Railway Stock Fund. The idea behind the Fund goes back to July 1967 when a group of railway enthusiasts in Hull visited the local wagonworks at Springhead. There they found a staff and tool van which had formerly been a Hull & Barnsley Railway bogie brake third carriage, a handsome looking vehicle in varnished teak livery when turned out by the Birmingham Railway Carriage & Wagon Company in 1912. Unfortunately its days of glory were long since past; panels were twisted or rotten, windows broken or boarded up, and indeed the vehicle had already been condemned by British Railways. But the enthusiasts considered it was worth per-serving as at that time no piece of rolling stock belonging to the former Hull & Barnsley Railway had been saved. When the Fund was formally established in March 1968 it was faced not only with the common problem of raising finance but also with the difficulty of finding a place where the coach could be stored safe from vandalism. The solution was a "marriage of convenience" between the Fund and the North Yorkshire Moors Railway which provided the former with a home for the vehicle within comparatively easy reach of Hull and the latter with much-needed rolling stock. Another similar coach has been located by the Fund at York; it too is a staff and tool van but is in good condition, has not been vandalised and is fitted with vacuum brakes. It could therefore be quickly made suitable for passenger train use and would prove a very useful asset. The Fund also hopes to purchase an open wagon from Tyne Commission Quay.

A further important vehicle on the line is a first class sleeping car bought from British Railways for £450 and at present used as a mobile base by week-end working parties. All rolling stock is now concentrated at Goathland, although at the time of writing it is not on public view. An important date was April 13th, 1969, when the first ballast train ran up the line as far as this point. Thus step by step work continues in the laborious process of nursing a railway back to full health and vigour. Slowly the weeds which have been growing unchecked between the tracks are being uprooted. Shrubs sprouting profusely on the slopes of embankments and cuttings are finding their growth nipped in the bud. Dereliction and decay is giving way to a tide of activity as the line regains a pride in its appearance.

Diesel rail bus at Castleton en route to Grosmont (John M. Boyes).

The Line Today

SUCH is the "progress" in present-day transport that to see the Whitby and Pickering Railway at best today requires a combination of train, car, well-heeled walking boots and even a pair of powerful binoculars. The first section from Whitby to Grosmont can be viewed in comparative ease and comfort by taking a seat at the front of one of the seven diesel units which depart on weekdays from Whitby for Middlesbrough via Battersby. The main change to Whitby station in recent years has been the loss of its overall roof in 1953, while the former dock outside the entrance has been filled in to become a car park. As the train nudges outside the station Whitby abbey is silhouetted against the sky on the left, and in the foreground the new Endeavour Wharf provides ample evidence that the town is again becoming a flourishing small seaport. Boat-building is a thriving craft at the yards on the opposite side of the Esk estuary, but one must be thankful that Whitby has retained much of its 18th century character through large-scale ship-building dying out before the most damaging years of the Industrial Revolution.

The line runs past the two-road engine shed which now has one entrance bricked up and is used as a warehouse, and on the other side it passes the goods depot, shorter than its original length as a result of being bombed in the last war. Nearby a circular pit denotes the site of the now vanished turntable. The town is left behind at the approach to Bog Hall Junction, once the scene of much activity with trains from Scarborough propelling down to Town station after crossing Esk viaduct and reversing at Prospect Hill Junction. Rusty rails still survive on this route as far as Hawsker, and may soon spring to life carrying block trains of potash.

Esk viaduct, 120-feet high with 12 arches, comes into view

as the tracks curve abruptly to the right. Just before the imposing red-brick spans a pile of rubble on the left is all that remains of the original railway weighing house, a once handsome building which ought to have been preserved. Immediately after the viaduct the railway passes the point where the Esk was diverted during the construction of the line, and then runs across low-lying land to enter Ruswarp station. Here all trains at one time stopped for tickets to be collected, and here too—in common with the other intermediate stations on the Whitby-Pickering line—delays were caused by trains having to draw-up twice owing to the shortness of the platforms.

Immediately past the station comes the first crossing of the Esk on a bridge which has a footpath running along its south side. Close at hand is the dam dividing tidal estuary from freshwater river. At this point the railway begins to climb on a gentle slope of 1 in 413, but apart from a very short stretch of 1 in 89 there are no really severe gradients all the way to Grosmont. The line hugs the east bank of the Esk as far as Sleights, a station that has lost its former profusion of seats and the level crossing at the east end which has been replaced by a well-proportioned girder bridge. The remaining $3\frac{1}{4}$ miles to Grosmont illustrate the way the Esk abruptly meanders with steep slopes alternating on opposite sides of the valley, thus forcing the railway to cross and re-cross the river on a

Old Whitby. Opposite page: A rather sombre view by Frank Sutcliffe of Town station about the turn of the century; the overall roof was removed in 1953. Above: View looking towards the abbey in the days of four-wheeled coaches (L&GRP).

series of bridges and providing the passenger with rapidly changing views.

About three-quarters of a mile from Sleights on the left side of the line are the ruins of the ancient chapel of St. John, built on the site of an old hermitage and becoming disused in 1767. Another quarter of a mile sees Woodlands Sidings trailing off on the right; these are the only lines still in situ out of a whole series of sidings up to Grosmont that once served past industries dotted along the slopes of the Esk Valley. Other features of note on this stretch include the cuttings through alum rock which caused so much difficulty during construction days, one of them being very close to the north bank of the river and not far from the point where the valley is so narrow that the railway has to be carried on an artificial ledge above the water.

There are absolutely no remains to be seen of Grosmont Priory, although when the new corn-shoots appear in spring-time the ground plan of the building is outlined by the varying shades of green. The Priory is sited alongside the railway near the last river-crossing before Grosmont station where the single Battersby line platform was a source of acute congestion in busier times. Opposite the platform a grass-grown area

55

denotes what was originally the site of the ironworks and later Hodsman's slag-crushing works. The exit from the station is by means of the down platform of the Whitby-Pickering line, and a quick look round reveals how successfully the efforts of the preservation society are keeping dereliction at bay. Alongside the present-day tunnel can be seen the original horse tunnel, now a footpath to some cottages. It can be reached by going through the small gate on the right immediately beyond the level crossing and then passing over the river by means of a footbridge replacing the original railway bridge dismantled in 1858. At the far end of the tunnel a depression in the ground indicates the site of a long-dismantled turntable which no doubt saw its heaviest period of use when the ironworks were in operation.

From Grosmont to Ellerbeck it should again soon be possible to enjoy the thrill of steam haulage, but in the meantime an attractive alternative is to explore both the original route and

Meeting of the ways near Goathland. The 1865 deviation line is in the foreground; the original 1836 alignment crosses the Cattle Arch in the left background before passing a former railway gatehouse (Harold D. Bowtell).

the deviation line on foot. From Grosmont the route is not through the horse tunnel, but once across the footbridge goes up past the church and then to the right as a stony track over the top of both tunnels. Careful watch is needed for a fieldpath which veers off through a small gate to the left and forms the way up the valley of the Murk Esk. As the path drops down to rail level there is a view of Deviation Junction signal box, closed about 1930, and then the hamlet of Esk Valley comes into view. The deviation line climbs away on the opposite side of the valley as the river nudges nearer to the original route at a point where the remains of Quarry Siding can still be discerned; from here a mineral line once crossed the Murk Esk and ran under the 1865 route to link up with a narrow gauge incline striding up the hillside to stone quarries on the fringe of Sleights Moor.

After the river temporarily meanders away to the left comes the site of Dowson Garth Siding, notable only for its heap of calcined ore from Beckhole Ironworks. A bridge over the fast-flowing water takes the old route on a course immediately parallel to but a hundred feet below the newer line which is here running on the edge of an almost sheer cliff. Then a gradual curve leads to the sunken hamlet of Beckhole, undeniably a beauty spot with its many spectacular waterfalls as well as the old incline cutting up through the trees. An original railway cottage is still standing at the foot of the incline, but the ironworks were demolished in the 1890s and the slag heaps used for road-making some 40 years later. The stepping stones over the beck formed of stone sleeper blocks from the original horse line are fascinating relics.

Railway cottages also survive at the top of the incline, and the one with a low-pitched roof—Ash Tree Cottage—was probably the original waiting room. It is but a short distance before the grassy track enters the scattered village of Goathland, green jewel in a moorland waste. Its claims to fame include the famous Plough Stotts; one of the oldest hunts in the country; a disproportionate number of hotels and boarding houses; strong associations with witchcraft; many ancient causeways; and a sprawling common almost splitting the moorland spa into a series of hamlets. The whole scene— ringed by heathery hills—has long been considered by many southerners as the embodiment of all that is best in Yorkshire, but the railway enthusiast will perhaps find greater inspiration at the almost idyllically sited station where two water cranes silently await the resumption of steam-hauled passenger services. Scarcely any traces remain of the stone crusher

The Rural Station:

There was something unique about the now almost-vanished country station, especially in the way periods of calm alternated with brief phases of unhurried activity. Opposite page, top: Sleights, which remains open for traffic from Whitby to Middlesbrough via the Esk Valley line (D. Hardy). Bottom: A 1939 view of picturesque Goathland with the stone crusher served by the narrow gauge tramway from Silhowe on the right (L&GRP). Above: Levisham, $1\frac{1}{2}$ miles from the village it purported to serve and out-of-sight of almost all signs of human habitation (F. K. Hickey).

which was fed by the narrow gauge tramway from Silhowe until the mines closed in 1948.

From the east side of the station a footpath heads back in the direction of Grosmont, providing a bird's-eye panorama of the once troublesome cutting on the deviation line. At Darnholm the path crosses Eller Beck, fine views being obtainable up and down the railway from the nearby overbridge towards picturesque Thomason Foss and the many rocky scars clothed with flowers. A series of tracks then lead across the moor to the Silhowe-Beckhole road, on which Braithwaite Farm marks the start of a lane dropping down to Green End hamlet overlooking both the original and the 1865 routes. Grosmont can be regained by going straight ahead along a path offering pleasing glimpses of the railway from clearings in a wood; it ultimately joins a wider track crossing the Murk Esk by two fords which make it necessary to deviate by way of Fair Head in times of wet weather.

The motorist holidaying in Whitby will find that a car is of only limited use in exploring the Whitby-Pickering railway, for remoteness from tarmac and exhaust fumes was always one of the most endearing characteristics of this line. From the harbour bridge it is best to take the Scarborough road until it veers sharply to the left and starts to climb; here turn right on to a minor road heading up towards Larpool from where the splendid roof-top vista over the town also provides perhaps the best view of the station. In the opposite direction it is possible to make a close-up, high level assessment of Esk viaduct before the road twists down to Ruswarp. Cross first the river by the imposing modern bridge and secondly the railway on the level at the south-west end of the station; then follow both the Esk and the twin line of rails on a closely parallel course to Sleights.

The Grosmont road goes off from the top end of the village at the foot of infamous Blue Bank, and averages a height of 250-feet above the railway which can be glimpsed in the valley bottom. From Grosmont it is necessary to return to the main Whitby-Pickering road on Sleights Moor, but on the way it is worth stopping close to the summit of Black Brow to have a look at Eskdaleside quarries. They were formerly connected to Eskdale Mines Sidings between Sleights and Grosmont by an incline, and both the winding house and a collapsed tunnel can still be seen. Stay on the main road for barely a quarter of a mile before turning right and right again to drop gradually down to Beckhole; the road crosses the railway and Eller Beck to climb up to Goathland on a course overlooking the

60

old incline.

After a glance at the station take the Pickering road which goes under the railway at Moorgates, a place of more than passing interest. It was on this stretch from Goathland that the railway cut the common in two, putting an end to days when it was possible to travel from the coast to the western edge of the Cleveland Hills without encountering a single wall or fence. To facilitate the movement of stock an attractive stone archway known as the Cattle Arch was built under the line at Moorgates, and a gatehouse erected in which a railwayman lived rent free in order to perform his duties. Both these structures survive as does the point where the original route merges with the deviation line.

The three colossal domes of Fylingdales Early Warning Station, looking like monstrous fuzz balls, loom over the horizon as the main road is rejoined. At the far side of a bridge on a sharp bend a footpath goes down to the North Riding County Council's Ellerbeck Siding, at present un-distinguished but likely soon to be a much busier place when it becomes—at least for the time being—the terminus of the North Yorkshire Moors Railway. Steam locomotives dating back to the Victorian era will be on almost nodding terms with the architecture of the supersonic age in its most frightening aspect.

Beyond Ellerbeck the Whitby and Pickering Railway may well have been reduced to a weed-infested track-bed by the time this book appears in print, but it will still not entirely be devoid of interest. Before retracing steps to the main road one should take a long but distant look at the forbidding Fen Bog and the entrance to Newtondale, once described as "in many ways the finest example of a glacial-lake overflow in England." Certainly it is among the most impressive of Yorkshire's Ice Age relics, being formed by the overspill from a huge lake eleven miles long and about 400 feet deep in Eskdale. Bracken, heather and the subtle colouring of the encircling moors combine to form an unforgettable scene.

One of the best views of Newtondale can be obtained by taking a walk of about half a mile from the main Whitby-Pickering road at Saltergate. The track starts near the *Wagon and Horses Inn,* a hostelry lying on an old pack-horse route used by salters carrying salt and alum from Cleveland and noted for its associations with smuggling as well as its peat fire which has reputedly burned continuously for 150 years. At Pifelhead the path ends on top of an almost sheer drop of over 200 feet to the dale floor, where the course of the line twists round rocky buffs like a writhing snake. Afforestation on the opposite slope is no longer endangered by fires started by steam locomotives pounding up a gradient in parts as steep as 1 in 50. Dominating the immediate horizon is Killingnoble Scar, a fine semi-circular range of rock once the haunt of a celebrated strain of hawks which were tended by local farmers under ancient law. At its foot Newtondale Well used to be the scene of strange rites at a fair held on Midsummer Sunday, while Needle Point is the name bestowed on a nearby rock with a perforated point.

Only one solitary road goes down to the actual floor of Newtondale, and this is a tortuous lane with Alpine-like gradients built solely to serve Levisham station. Turn off the Whitby-Pickering road three miles from Saltergate and then take extra care in negotiating the slopes of the ravine-like valley which separates the villages of Lockton and Levisham. Once the latter village has been reached there is still a distance of $1\frac{1}{2}$ miles and a descent of 300 feet to be covered before arriving at the station, a place possessing almost magical qualities in its apparent remoteness from all habitation. Yet less than half a mile away on the plateau above the west side of the valley is Newton, out of sight and until recently accessible from the dale floor only by a narrow zig-zag path. An amusing anecdote in Oswald Harland's *Yorkshire North Riding* relates how the author arrived at Levisham station in 1920 with a huge trunk, and thought he had indeed come to the end of the world when told that his destination of Newton could only be gained by a treacherous climb of 350-feet. He eventually paid the station-master's two boys five shillings to lug the trunk up the path.

From Newton a track goes down to The Grange, formerly *Raindale Inn,* where horses were changed during the early days of the railway. Two features of which only remnants remain are Raindale Siding and Raindale Mill—an ancient building with a wooden overshot waterwheel, moved stone by stone to form a working exhibit at York Castle Museum. On the return to the main road it is possible to give the legs a further extended stretch by taking the mile walk past Levisham church to Farwath (Farworth in railway spelling) which boasts

Opposite page:- Changes at Pickering. Top: A pre-war view with a train of clerestory coaches waiting to enter the platform (Raymond Hayes). Bottom: Ten years after the removal of the overall roof, a stopping train arrives at a rather bare-looking station in 1962 (W. R. Mitchell).

a pair of early lineside cottages and a little-used crossing. Sidings once trailed into a small quarry, while on the opposite hillside can be seen the medieval dike forming part of Blansby hunting park.

One of the few places at which the main road comes close to the railway is at Kingthorpe, two miles from Pickering, where recent tree felling affords a superb view up Newtondale with the distinctive rosebay willow-herb showing up against the russet bracken and serried ranks of pines. In Pickering itself the station is now very forlorn; the overall roof was removed in 1952, the small single-road engine shed has been disused since 1959, and the once fine station gardens might never have existed. It is a sorry picture. The enthusiast should not become so dispirited as to neglect a visit to Newbridge (on the Newton road) from where a two-foot gauge tramway formerly extended for two miles through Gundale Woods to quarries near Cawthorn. It originally had a Kerr Stuart saddle tank but from 1937 was worked by diesel and petrol locomotives until its closure in September 1961.

From Pickering the quickest return route to Whitby is by the main road, but diehard railway lovers will find an attractive alternative is to go up Rosedale, inspect the remains of the ironstone line and then head over Egton Moor to Egton Bridge and the Middlesbrough-Whitby road.

The narrow gauge Silhowe tramway entering a level.

In Conclusion

MANY a time must the fervent prayer have been muttered in Whitby that all copies of the Beeching Report be consigned to a soggy end in Fen Bog. With the benefit of hindsight it seems that the Report, and those who acted on its recommendations, were frequently guilty of allowing paper deficits to obscure all social and human issues. Whitby-Pickering, perhaps more than any other railway in the country, was a line that should never have closed.

Fen Bog is a memorial to the folly of a policy which sees edicts issued at national level without any real consideration of local issues. For south of this point the line is dead, leaving only skeletal remains for future reincarnation. And between Whitby and Grosmont it suffers the indignity of surviving solely to feed its younger off-shoot—the straggling branch to Battersby now fulfilling the role of the tail which wags the dog.

It is easy to argue that after a long life of 130 years the Whitby and Pickering Railway should be allowed to die peacefully: that preservation will either prolong the agonies or create a line so radically different as to be totally divorced from its predecessor. But this is to ignore one of the key purposes of the scheme—to cater for the needs of the community and the economy of the area by providing an essential train service for both residents and visitors. The North Yorkshire Moors Railway Preservation Society is no gathering of men playing with puffers nor will the railway be simply an outdoor museum of rusty relics. It would rather be thought of as an organisation dedicated to seeing the reinstatement of a transport facility which ought never to have been withdrawn. Exciting days lie ahead as this aim evolves into reality.

Interior of Goathland signal cabin (Tindale's of Whitby).

Maps

THE following six pages of maps depict the Whitby and Pickering Railway in its various aspects. Page 68 is a picture map drawn by Marie Hartley showing the line and its setting—the famous neighbouring features such as Lilla Cross, Wade's Causeway and Saltergate. Edward Jeffrey drew the map on page 69 to indicate the present extent of the North Yorkshire Moors Railway Preservation Society scheme from Grosmont to Ellerbeck and the track-bed which has been acquired by the Society right through to Pickering High Mill. The detailed maps of the line on pages 70 - 73 are by Judith Joy, and show respectively: Whitby to Eskdale Mines Sidings (near Grosmont); Eskdale Mines Sidings to Ellerbeck; Ellerbeck to Levisham; Levisham to Pickering.

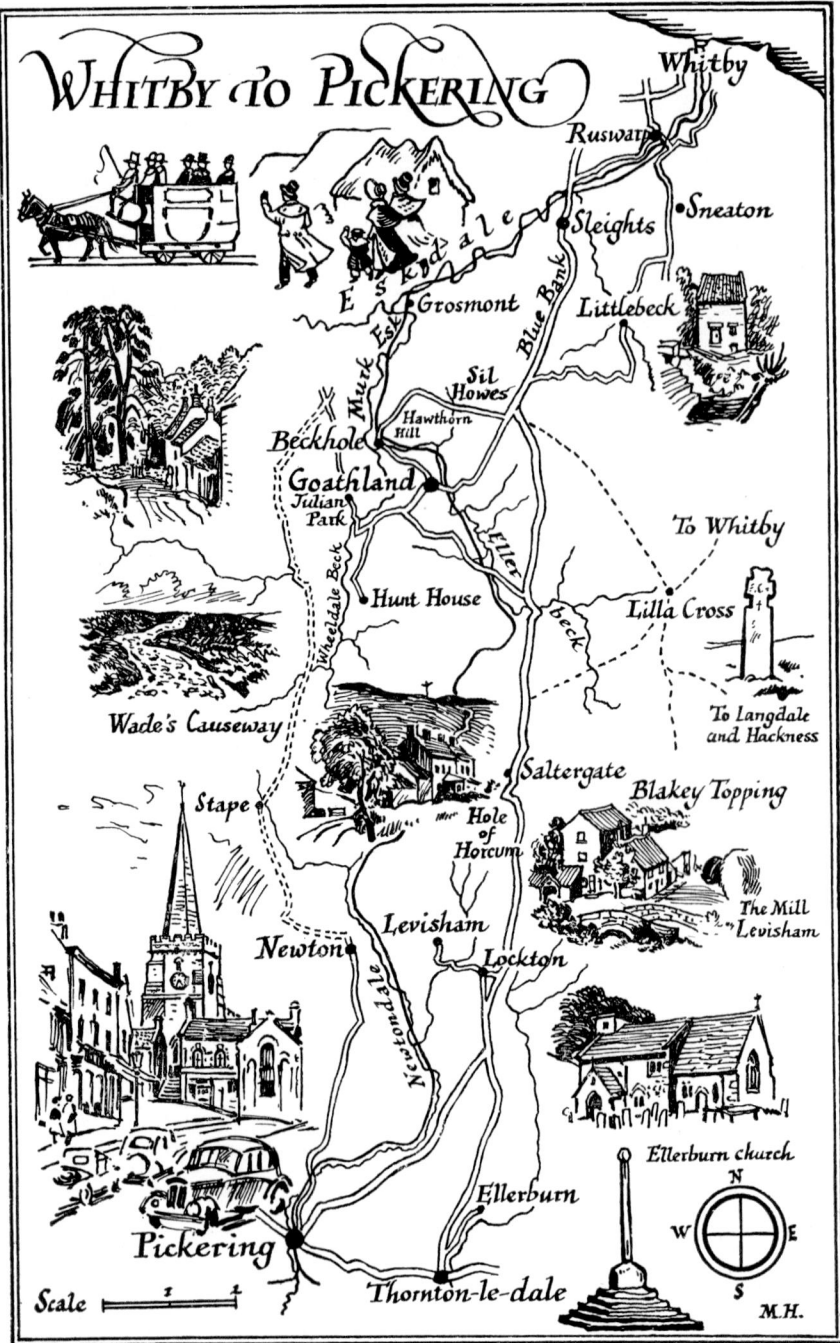

Whitby to Pickering

Whitby

Ruswarp

Sneaton

Sleights

Eskdale

Grosmont

Littlebeck

Murk Esk dale

Blue Bank

Sil Howes

Hawthorn Hill

Beckhole

Goathland

Julian Park

To Whitby

Wheeldale Beck

Hunt House

Eller beck

Lilla Cross

Wade's Causeway

To Langdale and Hackness

Saltergate

Blakey Topping

Stape

Hole of Horcum

The Mill Levisham

Levisham

Newton

Lockton

Newtondale

Ellerburn church

Pickering

Ellerburn

Thornton-le-dale

Scale

N
W   E
S

M.H.

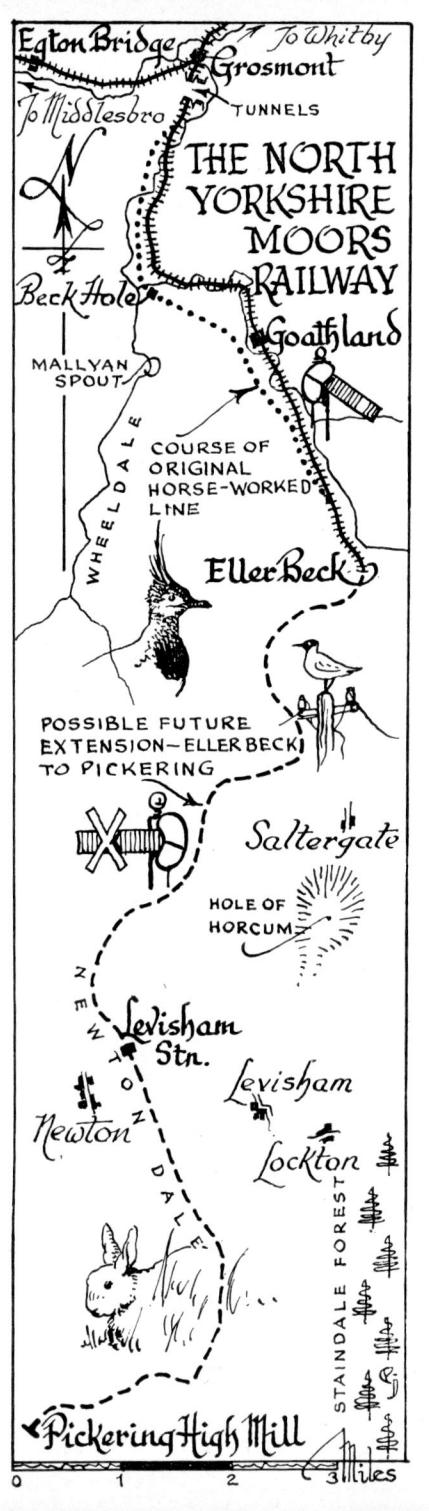

THE NORTH YORKSHIRE MOORS RAILWAY

Egton Bridge

To Whitby

Grosmont

To Middlesbro

TUNNELS

Beck Hole

Goathland

MALLYAN SPOUT

WHEELDALE

COURSE OF ORIGINAL HORSE-WORKED LINE

Eller Beck

POSSIBLE FUTURE EXTENSION—ELLER BECK TO PICKERING

Saltergate

HOLE OF HORCUM

Levisham Stn.

Levisham

Newton

Lockton

NEWTONDALE

STAINDALE FOREST

Pickering High Mill

0   1   2   3 Miles

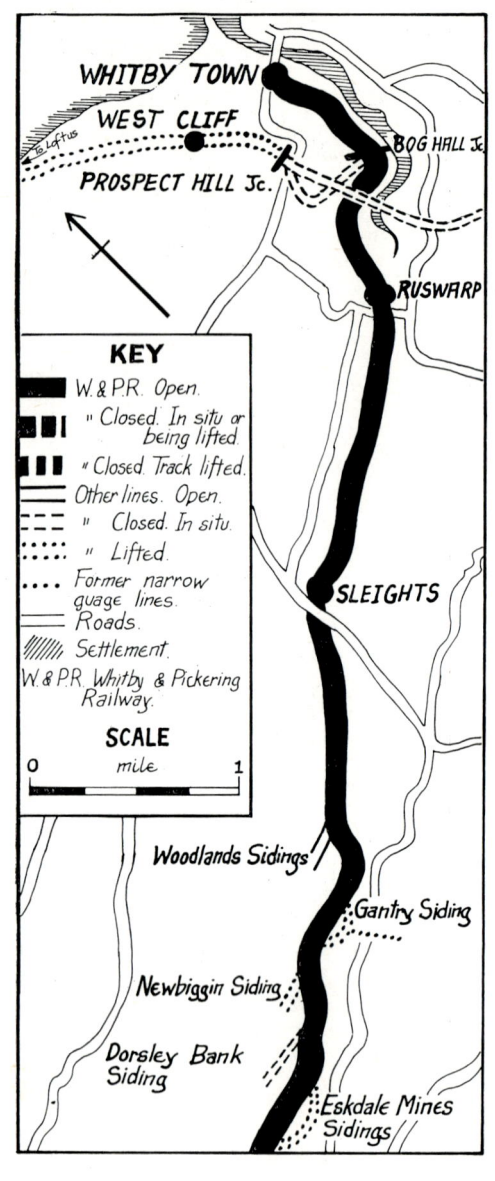

KEY

W. & P.R. Open.
" Closed. In situ or being lifted.
" Closed. Track lifted.
Other lines. Open.
" " Closed. In situ.
" " Lifted.
Former narrow guage lines.
Roads.
Settlement.

W. & P.R. Whitby & Pickering Railway.

SCALE

0   mile   1

WHITBY TOWN

WEST CLIFF

to Loftus

PROSPECT HILL Jc.

BOG HALL Jc.

RUSWARP

SLEIGHTS

Woodlands Sidings

Gantry Siding

Newbiggin Siding

Dorsley Bank Siding

Eskdale Mines Sidings

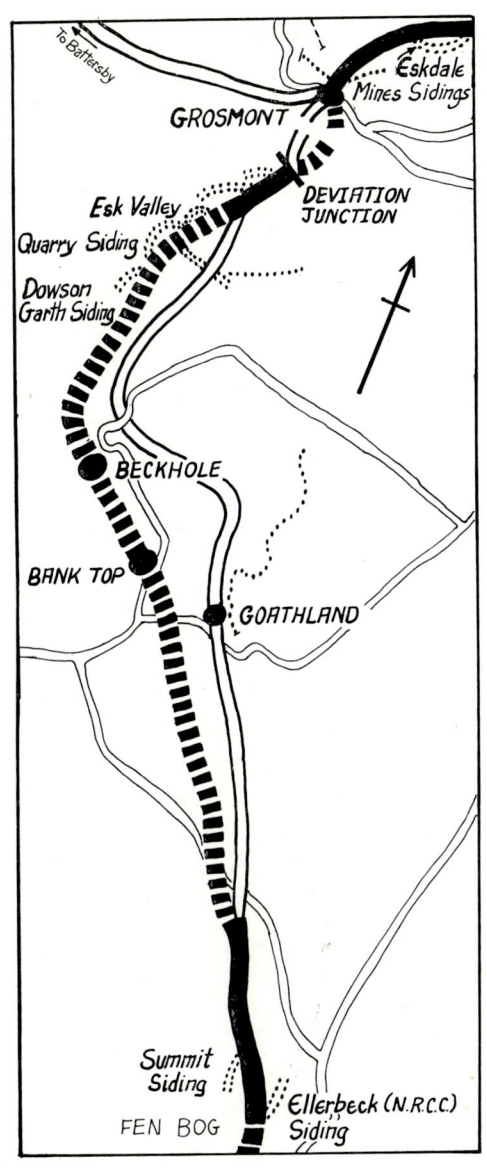

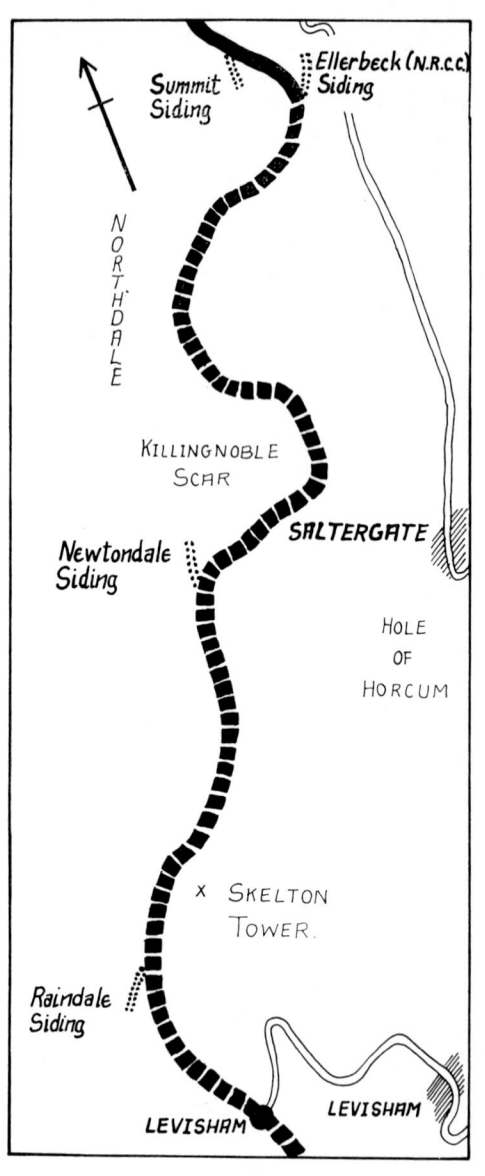

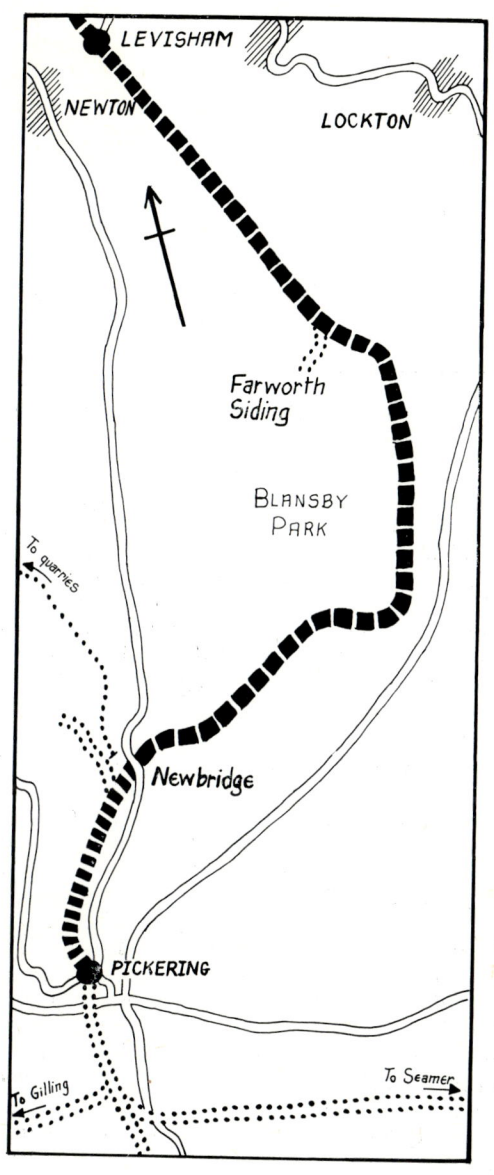

LEVISHAM

NEWTON

LOCKTON

Farworth
Siding

BLANSBY
PARK

To quarries

Newbridge

PICKERING

To Gilling

To Seamer

73

Further Reading

THERE have been two previous books devoted solely to the Whitby-Pickering line. *The Scenery of the Whitby and Pickering Railway* was published in 1836 to commemorate the opening of the route and publicise the district. Today it is useful not so much for the flowery text by Henry Belcher, a Whitby solicitor, but more for the excellent illustrations by George Dodgson who was apprenticed to Stephenson and prepared the plans for the line. Thirteen steel engravings and eight woodcuts provide a unique impression of a horse-worked railway in its setting. An appendix giving a contemporary description of the opening ceremony is also of value. Copies of this book are now hard to come by, but a reprint is under consideration.

Seventy years elapsed before the appearance of *A History of the Whitby and Pickering Railway* by G. W. J. Potter. With its high-quality illustrations complementing a detailed account of all aspects of the line, it is a work which can scarcely be faulted, the only possible criticisms being the occasional tendency towards "scissors and paste" composition and the poor maps. For a long time the book had been virtually unobtainable, but in 1969 it was reprinted by S. R. Publishers with an introduction by K. Hoole correcting the small number of errors and a postscript by G. D. Calvert bringing the story up to date.

W. W. Tomlinson's monumental and extremely accurate *North Eastern Railway: Its Rise and Development* (reprinted by David & Charles, 1967) covers the early stages in the promotion and development of the line in considerable depth, but events after the conversion to locomotive haulage are not described in detail. A complementary work, setting the development of the area's railways against their economic and social background, is *A Regional History of the Railways of Great Britain: Vol. 4, North East England* by K. Hoole (David & Charles, 1965). A fascinating chapter on the railway and its associations with Goathland, based partly on local anecdote, is contained in *Goathland in History and Folk-Lore* by F. W. Dowson (A. Brown & Sons, 1947).

George Hudson and George Stephenson have both been the subjects of good biographies—respectively *The Railway King* by Richard S. Lambert (2nd impression, Allen & Unwin, 1964) and *George and Robert Stephenson* by L. T. C. Rolt (Longmans Green, 1960). There are many general works on the area; recent studies are *North York Moors National Park* edited by Arthur Raistrick (H.M.S.O., 1966); *Yorkshire Ports and Harbours* by Baron F. Duckham (Dalesman, 1967); and *Yorkshire Coast* by Barrie Farnill (Dalesman, 1968).

Useful magazine articles include:- *The Whitby and Pickering Railway* by G. W. J. Potter (Railway Magazine, August 1900); *The Whitby and Pickering Railway* by C. M. Doncaster (Railway Magazine, August 1936); *The Whitby - Pickering - Malton Line of the North Eastern Railway* by K. Hoole (Trains Illustrated, September 1952); *Farewell to the Line down Newton Dale* by Malcolm Barker (York and County, 1965); *When Locos had Legs* by Mervyn Brown (Yorkshire Life, March 1966); *The North Yorkshire Moors Railway, etc.*, by G. D. Calvert (reprint from York and County, 1968); *The Battle for Grosmont - Pickering* by Howard Hazell (Yorkshire Life, January 1969); *Re-birth of a North Yorkshire Railway* by David Joy (The Dalesman, April 1969). Newsletters published about every three months by the North Yorkshire Moors Railway Preservation Society are the best source of present developments on the line.

Index

76

NORTH YORKSHIRE MOORS
RAILWAY PRESERVATION SOCIETY

Secretary: T. Salmon, Esq., "Rosebank", The Avenue, Ruswarp, Whitby, North Yorkshire.

ANNUAL MEMBERSHIP FEES

Adult	£1 – 0 – 0
Husband and wife	£1 – 10 – 0
Pensioner or young person (under 18) ..	10 – 0
Business Members	£5 – 0 – 0
Corporate Members (Schools, Societies)	£3 – 0 – 0

Life Members	£15 – 0 – 0
	(or three instalments of £5)
Life Members (Pensioners)	£7 – 10 – 0

Members receive a quarterly Newsletter and will be entitled to reduced fares, and have the opportunity of assisting the Society in its many departments by their voluntary services. Business members are also entitled to advertising space in Society journals. In several parts of the country Area Groups have been formed, which hold meetings in the area and assist in the arrangement of working parties.

NORTH YORKSHIRE MOORS
RAILWAY PRESERVATION SOCIETY

Debenture

The prospectus for the North Yorkshire Moors Railway Ltd. Debenture (First Issue) will be ready shortly. The issue will be in units of £10 and will be available to members.

Yard of Track

For £3 you can become the "owner" of a yard of track and have your name inscribed on a sleeper. Send for details to the Fund Raising Officer:- C. Hart, Esq., 1, Suspension Bridge, Ruswarp, Whitby, North Yorkshire.

Have you relatives or friends abroad?
Then tell them about our special

Overseas Membership

which includes

Life Membership of the Society
Free travel on the railway
"Ownership" of a yard of track
and a free copy of this book

Further details of the Society's activities can be obtained from the Secretary.

Newton Dale.